I THINK GOD IS GAY

BY

SIPHO ELLEN TSHAKA

I Think God Is Gay

Copyright @2020 by Sipho Ellen Tshaka. All rights reserved. Published and Printed in the Republic of South Africa.

No part of this book may be reproduced by any mechanical, electronic or photographic process, or transmitted in any form or otherwise be copied for public or private use, without prior permission of the publisher.

ISBN: 978-0-620-90741-5

Published by: tshakasipho1@gmail.com

FRESH MIND
PUBLICATIONS

I Think God Is Gay

...I know you might have picked up this book out of spit, or out of anger because of its tittle. Maybe you are just an amazing reader, and you are interested in reading my work as well, or you are just curious, whatever motivated you to choose this book, thank you. I promise you it was not a mistake, and you will not regret it.

To those who feel offended by the tittle, I am so sorry if it's painful, but that alone should tell you something about yourself but let me not judge you. Can you at least try to read till the end and give yourself time and a chance to understand the content before you crucify me because of a cover and words. *"Don't judge the book by its cover"*, remember that phrase. Anyway, thank you for choosing me. It's an honour.

To my Hero, the big guy, God. Thank you, you are indeed beyond what words alone

I Think God Is Gay

could ever manage, keep doing your miracles, keep showing up for everyone. You are amazing, and for that alone, you deserve a place in our hearts.

To my sister, my shiro, my anchor, my mirror. You have carried my spirit when I was too weak to lift it myself. You've listened to my cries, challenged my thoughts, and held me through moments that tried to break me. You have been the loudest reminder that love can be unconditional. That family, when it chooses to love without restraint, is the closest thing to God.

To my mother, the quiet strength in my bones. You have loved me even when you didn't fully understand me. You have stood beside me when others stood against me. You taught me that support doesn't always need explanation, that sometimes, the purest love simply says, "I'm here." Thank

I Think God Is Gay

you for showing me that faith and love can live in the same room, even when they don't always speak the same language.

To every soul who made me feel unworthy, thank you. You made me search deeper for the truth of who I am. You made me brave enough to write this. And to you, reader, thank you for picking up this book. Thank you for daring to feel. For daring to question. For daring to believe that maybe love was always the gospel.

This is not the end of my story. It's the beginning and I hope you will stick around with me.

To you, yes, you, who felt a shiver, a glimpse of joy in your insides when you first look at this book. You are free, God is you and life is yours to enjoy, get on it and keep moving.

I Think God Is Gay

To everyone else, please take it easy and allow the Divine to bless you with eternal Bliss. And please relax, we are all Gay. Yes, we are all Gay, even you.

I Think God Is Gay

INTRODUCTION

We live in a world where everything we think we know is a breath away from breaking. Where the truth is elastic, and certainty is a luxury. One moment, you're told the world is round and full of wonder, and the next, it flattens beneath the weight of someone else's belief system. We live in a world built on rules that no longer rule, where right and wrong shapeshift based on culture, country, skin colour, gender, and who you dare to love.

Somehow, even in this chaos, we still look up. Still ask questions. Still pray. Still hope. Still try to be "good."
But what does good even mean anymore?

We were raised on scripts, fed sermons like medication, taught to fear fire before we ever felt warmth. We were told God is love, omnipresent, omnipotent, the great I AM,

I Think God Is Gay

but only if we colour within the lines. God loves you, they said. Unless you're gay. God forgives you, they said. Unless you're too different. Too loud. Too feminine. Too much. God sees you, they said. But only if you kneel, repent, suppress, and conform.

We were born with questions, but punished for asking them.

Let's talk about that God.
Let's talk about the image of God we were handed, like a weapon disguised as a cross. Let's talk about the contradictions dressed up as doctrine.
Let's talk about how a book meant to liberate became a tool of shame, and how people use God to control, exclude, and hate, then dare to call it holy.

They say God is all-loving, and yet we live in a world cracked by hatred.
They say God is all-powerful, and yet

I Think God Is Gay

children starve while pulpits grow fat with gold.

They say God is merciful, and yet a boy in a dress can be beaten and left for dead with "Leviticus" carved into his flesh.

They say God made us in His image, but some of us are still called abominations for loving who we love or becoming who we are.

They tell us to worship a God who seems to have lost interest in justice, unless that justice is aimed at the already broken.

They say God sacrificed His only son to save the world, and then tell us we're still going to hell for being born different.

We sing hymns to a saviour nailed to a tree but ignore the crucifixions happening every day to those who don't fit the mould. And when life hurts, when the prayer isn't answered, when the healing doesn't come, when the church turns its back, we're told

I Think God Is Gay

it's our fault. We didn't pray hard enough. We weren't faithful enough. We didn't believe enough.

God becomes the monster we made Him.

But I ask this:
What if God isn't who we were taught to believe?
What if God is *gayer, bi or more of a lesbian* than we dared to imagine?
What if God exists beyond the binary, beyond the stained-glass windows, beyond the judgmental sigh of a preacher on Sunday morning?
What if God is not just in the heterosexual white Jesus portrait hanging in church halls, but in the trans child in Cape Town, the gay teenager in Jozi, the drag queen in Durban, the lesbian mother in Gqeberha?

What if God is not ashamed of us, but is actually *in us*?

I Think God Is Gay

What if God is gay?

Before you throw the book across the room, hear me.

I'm not saying God is bound by any sexuality or gender identity, we can't reduce the Divine to human categories. But I am saying this: if God truly created us in Their image, then LGBTQI+ community people are not just tolerated, they are reflections of the Divine. If God *is* love, as the Bible says, then every form of love, freely given, honestly expressed, authentically lived, is holy. And if God is with the oppressed, the marginalized, the ridiculed, and the crucified... then wouldn't God be closer to the ones thrown out of churches than the ones throwing?

This book is not a theology textbook. It's not a gospel remix. It's my story. It's my wound. It's my healing. It's my life.
It's the scream of someone who begged God

I Think God Is Gay

to fix them before realizing they were never broken.

It's the echo of every queer soul who whispered "Do you still love me?" into the dark, and got silence in return.

It's a rebellion against a version of God that only shows up for straight people.

It's a resurrection of the God I had to go searching for, the one I eventually found hiding under all the shame, standing in a rainbow robe, arms wide open.

This is not just a book. It's a funeral for the God who was too small. And it's a birth. A dangerous, liberating birth.

So, if you're still holding this book, it means you're ready. Or at least curious. And that's enough.

Welcome. Let's talk.

I Think God Is Gay

Born into the Church

I was born into the rhythm of gospel hymns and whispered prayers. Into a world where the name "Jesus" carried more weight than any truth I might discover on my own. Where Sunday was sacred, not because it offered rest, but because it demanded devotion.

Every Sunday, like clockwork, my mother's voice would pierce the morning air with a firm, loving command:

"It's time to show our appreciation to the Lord. Makuyiweni maqabani, vukani" she would say.

That was her way of saying we were going to church. No questions, no objections. You dressed up, you looked sharp, and you smiled, no matter how you felt. Your clothes didn't have to be expensive, but they had to be clean. Your attitude had to be grateful.

I Think God Is Gay

Even if you hadn't eaten the night before, even if your father was absent, even if life made no sense, you still had to show up and give thanks.

That was the contract we never signed but were born into. And I followed it like my life depended on it. Because, in many ways, I believed it did.

I believed, as I was taught, that if I missed church, something terrible would happen to me. That skipping service meant inviting curses into my future. That God's blessings had attendance requirements. That if I didn't kneel low enough, clap loud enough, or believe hard enough, I would never be successful. That my life would rot before it even began.

I was told that God was watching. Not with kindness, but with surveillance. That every lie, every mistake, every stray thought could

I Think God Is Gay

tip the scales of heaven. That God was not just a saviour; He was a judge with a long memory and a short fuse.

Don't lie.
Don't steal.
Don't speak ill of others.
Be kind, even when others are cruel.
Obey, even when the rules don't make sense.
Give, even when you have nothing left.

Because if you don't, they said, you'll go to hell.

Hell. That was the word used to keep me afraid. It was the place they promised I'd end up if I ever stepped outside the holy box, they built around me. And I wanted to be good. I tried to be good. I tried to be the kind of child who pleased God. I memorized the verses, sang the songs, prayed the prayers. I stood in front of the

I Think God Is Gay

church and said how great God had been to me, even when I wasn't sure what that meant. Even when I was hurting. Even when I was confused. Because doubt had no place in the pews.

They said God was amazing. Huge. Mighty. The Father above the sky. He created the world, parted the seas, defeated giants, and raised the dead. He was a God of miracles. A God of promises. A God who made a way, if only you had faith.

But my faith kept running into a wall. Because the world I saw didn't look like the stories I was told. I saw people dying, young, innocent, praying people. And God was there. Silent.

I saw pastors take offerings from the poor and build empires. Women gave their last coin in hope and died with nothing but a

I Think God Is Gay

receipt of their belief. Where were the blessings?

I saw kids stealing shoes from outside the church door while we shouted "Hallelujah!" inside.

I saw congregants clap while gossiping about the woman in the third row with the short dress. I saw smiles that vanished the moment the sermon ended. I saw people pretending. And I learned to pretend, too.

I had a father. Sort of. He was never really home. I prayed for him, night after night, asking God to bring him back. But he didn't. Instead, he died before I even started school. I was five. God, they said, was still watching. Still loving. Still in control.

I didn't understand that kind of love. I still don't. Love that only takes and gives pain.

They said God is always at work, even when you can't see Him. They said He

I Think God Is Gay

moves in the shadows, that He comes when you least expect Him. But what kind of God hides when a child is crying? What kind of God only shows up when it's convenient for Him?

The truth is, I was born in church, but I never found freedom there. I found fear. I found performance. I found expectation. I found a ladder to climb with no top, no rest, no real reward.

They kept asking for more. More money. More time. More faith.
They said, "*God blesses those who give.*"
But what if I had nothing to give?
What if all I had was the question lodged in my throat: *Does God love poor people less?*
And if I didn't give, would God ignore me? Would He let me suffer to teach me a lesson?

I Think God Is Gay

This is what nobody wants to say out loud: The version of God I was given looked suspiciously like the people who benefitted from my silence. God loved the givers, the tithers, the obedient. God blessed the pastors, the "men of God," the ones who spoke loudest. But the rest of us? The kids with nothing to offer but brokenness, queerness, confusion and gay? We were the projects. The sinners. The ones who needed fixing. And here's the irony of God, at least the way they painted Him:

He creates you.
He knows you.
He designs your heart, your desires, your body.
And then, if you mess up, if you *sin*, He punishes you.
He threatens you with eternal fire.
He sets the rules, then dares you to fail.

I Think God Is Gay

I was born into the church, but I wasn't born free. I was born into a place that was supposed to offer salvation but ended up teaching me shame. And still, I kept believing in something greater. Not because the sermons convinced me, but because the ache in my soul refused to go numb.

Maybe I'm not the perfect believer. Maybe I don't pray like I used to. Maybe I question more than I should. But I still believe.

Not in the God, they gave me, but in a God I have yet to fully understand. A God who is bigger than church.
A God who doesn't demand perfection before love.
A God who walks with the ones religion has left behind.

A God who just might be gay.

I Think God Is Gay

Whispers in the Dark

When I was a child, before they edited the Bible into glossy new translations and politically palatable verses, they said God created us. All of us. And only two of us, *male and female*. Simple, clean, binary. That's what they preached from the pulpit. That was the framework. Two genders. Two destinies. Two boxes you were forced into whether you fit or not.

I remember those words like gospel bullets shot into my brain before I even knew what they meant:

"He made them male and female."
"A man shall not lie with another man."
"The effeminate shall not inherit the Kingdom of God."

It was doctrine. It was law. It was weaponized in every sermon that danced near the subject of sex, identity, or

I Think God Is Gay

queerness (LGBTQI+). There was no room for questioning, only obedience. They said being gay was the greatest abomination, that same-gender love was filth birthed in the pits of hell. They said it was demonic. They said it was rebellion. They said it was Satan, wearing a pride flag, walking in stilettos, smiling with a forked tongue.

But if God created everything...
If God saw it all and called it good...
Then tell me, *where was God when I was created? When the gayness grew stronger?*

Was He distracted the day I was formed in the womb?
Did the Devil slip something into the spiritual gene pool when no one was looking? Why would God make me this way if He intended to punish me for it?

Those are the questions I asked. I didn't scream them. I whispered them. In private.

I Think God Is Gay

In prayer. In trembling. And when I finally gathered the courage to ask them out loud, to someone I trusted in church, they didn't answer.

They expelled me.

Not officially, no paperwork, no formal announcement. Just cold glances, awkward silences, whispered warnings behind my back.
"You're confusing the other children."
"You're playing with spirits you don't understand."
"You're opening doors to demons."

All I did was ask:

"Where was God when I was made?"
And it costed me my place at the altar.

That was the day I realized something terrifying: The Church has no mercy for the child who questions. The church has no

I Think God Is Gay

home for the heart that doesn't fit the mould.

The deeper I leaned into God, the further I felt from Him. And the more I tried to belong, the more I became a ghost. A quiet contradiction in the corner pew. And then came the rumours, the ones that shattered what little innocence I had left.

They said two women pastors, yes, pastors, were "intimate." But not *gay*, they said. No, no, not *that*. They were just "spiritually connected." They were so united in the Holy Spirit that when they were together, they heard the voice of God more clearly. They performed miracles. They spoke in tongues. They delivered demons, together.

But let's not call it *gay*. Let's never say that, maybe their love, however complicated, could be *real*. Let's bend theology into whatever shape it needs to be, just as long

I Think God Is Gay

as it doesn't look like queerness. Let's justify it in holy language. Let's erase the truth with spiritual metaphors.

And my head... my head nearly exploded. Because if *they* could be intimate and still be accepted, then what did that mean for me? Why is it that same-gender affection is only acceptable when it's wrapped in church clothing?

If you love a woman and you're a woman, that's demonic.
But if you love her *in the Spirit*, if it helps the church grow, then it's divine?

The lines didn't make sense.
None of it made sense, unless you made the rules yourself. And I realized: that's what religion had become. A personalized rulebook. A kingdom of convenience.

The God I was taught to worship, He had been fragmented, sliced, and served to

I Think God Is Gay

people based on power, performance, and preference.

But I wasn't given that luxury. I didn't fit into their God-box. I didn't even have a label to hold.

See, I didn't grow up feeling attracted to men or women. I didn't feel arousal. I didn't feel desire. Not the way others did. I thought maybe I was broken. Maybe I was late. Maybe I just hadn't "found the right one."

So, I told someone, someone I thought I could trust in church. She looked at me with pity, like I had been touched by darkness. She said, *"That's the Devil confusing you."* She told me to pray. Hard. For seven days. No food, just fasting. Cry out to God. And He would "heal" me. She said if I didn't change, if I didn't become "normal," I would go to hell.

I Think God Is Gay

But what kind of God lets a child suffer silently and calls it sin?

What kind of God watches a confused teenager beg for identity and stays silent? And what kind of church tells a soul like mine that I am only worthy if I become someone else?

I was praying. I was fasting. I was reading scripture. I was on my knees.
So, how did the Devil get in? If God is all-powerful, all-knowing, and so loving, then how was I still broken in His presence?

They didn't have answers. Just commands.
Pray more.
Obey more.
Change.

But what if there was nothing wrong with me to begin with?

What if the only sin was believing that I had to erase myself to earn divine love?

I Think God Is Gay

I wonder why God made me this way.
I wonder if He did it on purpose.
I wonder if He is waiting for me to stop apologizing.

I wonder if God gets tired of watching His name be used as a weapon. Because these whispers in the dark, these quiet truths that live in the cracks of scripture and silence,
They don't go away.
They grow louder with every fake smile, every quiet shame, every religious performance.

And maybe, just maybe...
Those whispers are God.
Trying to tell me that I was never the mistake.

That the mistake was ever believing love had to look one way.

I Think God Is Gay

Praying the Gay Away

Have you ever felt trapped between your soul and your skin? Like your heart beats in one direction, but your mind is tied to an altar that was never built for you? I have. For years. I prayed the gay away. Every single night, I folded my hands and pleaded with the God they told me loved me, but only if I changed. I asked Him to make me normal. To make me right. To fix me.

It started softly, like all traumas do. With a whisper. A glance. A sense that I was different, not because I felt like I had a curse inside me, but because the people I trusted told me I did. They said it with smiles on their faces and verses on their tongues. They wrapped their homophobia in scripture and handed it to me like a gift, a righteous act of concern for my eternal soul.

I Think God Is Gay

I believed them. Of course I did. I was young, obedient, and terrified of hell.

They told me God was love, but somehow, I was outside of that love. They told me I had to fast, to cry out, to kneel until my knees bruised, and maybe then God would scrape the sin from my soul like a stain too shameful to name.

So, I tried. I gave it everything.

I became the best version of what they wanted. I was the perfect worshiper. My prayers? Loud and bold. My hands? Always lifted. My Bible? Worn and underlined. I danced. I sang. I cried real tears. I prayed in tongues I didn't understand, hoping it would unlock the gates of Heaven just enough to let me in, not as I was, but as they needed me to be.

But nothing changed.

I Think God Is Gay

I didn't become straight. I didn't suddenly desire the things they told me I should. I didn't wake up with a new appetite for "normal." Instead, I woke up hollow. Cold. Numb. While everyone else shouted and claimed their breakthrough, I sat in the back, drowning in silence.

I thought I was broken. I thought maybe I had been born with the wrong soul, or maybe I had missed the boat to Heaven and was stuck wandering in a body that even God regretted making.

They never told me that spiritual abuse feels like betrayal coated in holy water. That the greatest sin is not loving someone of the same gender, but convincing someone that their love is unholy. That their heart is unworthy.

I remember fasting for seven days, just like they told me. No food. No water. Just

I Think God Is Gay

prayer and pain. I was desperate to be fixed. I wanted so badly to please God. But deep down, I think I was more afraid of the people in the pews than I was of any eternal damnation. Because the church didn't just preach fire and brimstone, they became it. And I was always the fuel.

One elder told me that my lack of sexual desires was proof that I was under demonic attack. That some spirit had latched itself to me and was devouring my natural instincts. They made me believe that I was a battlefield for God and Satan. That my body was not my own. They never once asked me how I felt. They never once looked me in the eye and said, "You are loved. You are whole. You are not a mistake." They were too busy playing saviours to remember how to be human.

So, I left.

I Think God Is Gay

I left one church and tried another. And another. And another. Different names. Different uniforms. Different rituals. But the same smell of shame followed me through every door.

They said, "God is good," but their eyes said, "You are wrong."

They said, "God is love," but their tone said, "Not for you."

They said, "All are welcome," but their silence said, "Don't speak your truth here."

Still, I searched. I kept looking. Not for another church, but for myself. Because maybe, just maybe, I wasn't the problem.

Maybe the problem was the system that worshiped a version of God too small to contain the diversity of His creation. Maybe the problem was the fear that told people to hate in the name of holiness. Maybe it wasn't me who needed saving, but the

I Think God Is Gay

institution that taught me to hate myself in the first place.

When I stopped reading the Bible and started reading books by people who dared to question, who dared to think for themselves, my soul began to breathe again.

Neale Donald Walsch. Bell Hooks. James Baldwin. Audre Lorde. People who wrote about God not as a dictator in the sky but as a presence, a pulse, a deep well of love that couldn't be contained by doctrine. A love that didn't require me to beg. A love that didn't ask me to change. For the first time, I started to believe in a God who looked like me. A God who understood complexity. A God who didn't flinch at my questions or run from my confusion. A God who was not male or female. A God who was not heterosexual or cisgender. A God who simply *was*.

I Think God Is Gay

A God who whispered to me: "*You are enough.*"

It took years to unlearn what the church taught me. Years to look in the mirror without hearing their voices in my head. Years to believe that love, real, messy, human love, is not a sin.

I still pray. But my prayers have changed.

I no longer ask God to fix me. I ask Him to help me stay alive. I ask Her to remind me that I matter. I ask Them to walk beside me through a world that often chooses fear over understanding.

I no longer try to pray the gay away. I pray for strength. For truth. For courage. And most of all, I pray for those still trapped in the pews, begging for salvation that will never come from a place that sees them as less than divine.

I Think God Is Gay

The God I Knew vs. The God I Felt

A few years ago, something happened to me. Something unexplainable, something sacred. I wish I had the perfect word for it, an emotion, an energy, a light. Some might call it instinct. Others, a sixth sense. The romantics would say it was love at first sight. But me? I just call it God.

Not the God they shouted about on the pulpit. Not the God wrapped in rules, guilt, and fear. Not the God who supposedly keeps a tally of my sins, waiting for me to slip so he can push me closer to hell. No, this was different. This wasn't the God I knew. This was the God I *felt*.

The God I knew was explained to me with fury and shame. He was presented as jealous and vengeful, with a narrow love that only extended to those who fit the mould. This God demanded weekly

I Think God Is Gay

attendance, tithes, and obedience, and if you deviated, even slightly, you were discarded, cast away, deemed a sinner.

They taught me about his love, but preached hatred for the different.
They said he was merciful, but he watched children suffer and did nothing. They said he was just, but unjust people rose in his name.
They said he loved me, but only if I wasn't gay, bi, trans, asexual, or confused.

The God they preached about gave rules without reason, punishments without understanding, and grace only to those who could afford to pretend they were perfect.

But that day, in that quiet moment, sitting on a sunlit bench outside a library helping some students with their assignments, I felt something so powerful I thought my chest would burst. No one had their hands raised.

I Think God Is Gay

No gospel was playing. There was no altar, no oil, no shouting. Just peace. Just presence. Just...God.

It was like the warmth of a thousand suns lived inside me. A current that flowed through my veins like molten light. I looked around at the world differently. I saw people, really saw them, flawed, tired, struggling, and I felt love. Real love. Not judgment dressed in prayer. Not pity disguised as grace. But an overwhelming compassion that demanded nothing in return. That was the God I *felt*.

I realized then that God isn't just a being sitting above the clouds tallying our rights and wrongs. God is an energy. A force. A consciousness that doesn't scream from pulpits but whispers in pain, in beauty, in kindness. God is the moment you give up your seat on a crowded bus without thinking. God is the silence that speaks

I Think God Is Gay

louder than words when you wipe away someone's tears. God is the ache you feel when you witness injustice, not because you were told it was wrong, but because your soul won't let it sit right with you.

That's the God I *felt*.

The God I knew never showed up when I needed him the most. He was always conditional, always out of reach. The God I knew needed me to dress a certain way, speak a certain way, and love a certain way. But the God I felt showed up uninvited, unexpected, and undeniable. In a moment of simplicity and service. While helping students' study. While giving without agenda. While loving without fear.

Years later, I felt him again. I was on a date with a young lady from the house of Sotuko. A woman I admired, someone kind and gentle and real. As we sat across from

I Think God Is Gay

each other, eating simple food and laughing about life, I felt that same divine energy rise in me. The warmth. The knowing. The sacredness of presence. Religion had taught me that dating was a sin. That loving anyone outside the blueprint of heterosexual marriage would cost me heaven. But God was there. With us. Smiling in the background. Laughing along. Breathing between us.

I knew in that moment that God wasn't angry. He wasn't warning me. He wasn't disappointed. He was present. Joyful. Comfortable.

I started to understand something they never taught me in church; God does not leave us. We leave God. When we trade love for judgment. When we silence our hearts for conformity. When we shame instead of embrace. When we pretend rather than live. That's when we step away from

I Think God Is Gay

God. But even then, God doesn't stop loving. He waits, like still water, for us to return.

I believe now that God is in everyone. Gay, straight, queer, trans, celibate, bi, or confused. God is not in labels. God is not in fear. God is not in shame. God is not a weapon to be used against someone else's truth. God is love, and love does not condemn.

I've stopped trying to make God fit into the Bible verses that were rewritten by kings and councils. I stopped trying to pray away who I am. I stopped trying to understand the contradictions of a God they controlled through religion. Instead, I now feel the God who is free. The God who is fire and light and softness and power. The God who walks with the broken. The God who sees me, as I am, and says, "I am in you. I never left."

I Think God Is Gay

The God I feel doesn't need praise to love. Doesn't need offerings to bless. Doesn't demand perfection to be present. This God simply *is*, and that is enough

I Think God Is Gay

Exile in the Sanctuary

There was once a time when the word "church" meant sanctuary, a sacred space to run to, not away from. It was supposed to be where the broken found healing, the lost found direction, the hated found love, and the guilty found grace. But in the world, I grew up in, the sanctuary was no longer sacred. It became a courtroom. And most of us were already sentenced before we walked through the door.

Angie was a flame, alive, bright, and proud. She wore her truth in her eyes, her freedom in her walk. But freedom wasn't welcome at church. One Sunday, she came in with a red weave and a skirt just above the knee. The whispers started in the back pew before the worship even began. They told her she was tempting the men, she was disrespecting the house of the Lord, she was leading the brethren into sin. As if the men's self-control

I Think God Is Gay

was her responsibility. As if holiness was stitched into the hemline of a skirt. They didn't care to hear her voice or feel her spirit. Angie stopped coming. She was exiled for being too much of herself in a place that claimed to worship a God who created all of her.

Sam was another story. A soft man with loud pain. He drank not to party, but to forget. To silence the screaming thoughts of a trauma he never had the tools to name. Yet he still came to church every Sunday, drunk, but present. Wanting. Hoping. But they mocked him. They'd wipe the pews after he sat. They'd pray over him like he was possessed, not broken. The pastor told him once to "come back when you're sober, and God can hear you then." But Sam needed God most in the moments he was drunk. They didn't see that. They only saw the bottle, not the boy still crying inside the

I Think God Is Gay

man. Eventually, Sam disappeared. Not because God left him, but because the people who claimed to know God pushed him out.

Tholekile never even had a chance. Her grandmother was rumoured to be a witch, a village whisper that grew into a roar. And by association, Tholekile was marked. Cursed. Dirty. Unfit to be among the children of God. She didn't do anything. No proof, no trial, no crime. Just bloodline. Just fear. Just ignorance wrapped in a holy robe. She was exiled. No farewells. No outreach. Just silence, cold and heavy.

And then there was Melikhaya. Quiet. Smart. Beautiful. But beneath the polished surface lived a secret that was too heavy to carry alone. He was gay. And in the church, that was enough to be considered a demon. So, he hid. He clapped when they clapped, he danced when they danced, and he

I Think God Is Gay

amen'd the very sermons that condemned him to Hell. He prayed harder than most because he thought maybe, just maybe, he could pray the gay away. But inside, he was dying. Hating himself. Asking God why He would make him this way if He truly loved him. And still, Melikhaya stayed silent. Because silence meant survival.

The sanctuary had become a prison. And slowly, the exiles became many.

Some of us were kicked out.
Others left quietly.
The rest of us stayed, but we were already gone on the inside.

So now, the pews are full, but the hearts are empty. The hands are lifted in worship, but the minds are thinking about who's watching. Church became theatre. A weekly audition for God's approval, but really for

I Think God Is Gay

the approval of people too broken to admit their own sin.

Now the youth go to church not to be transformed, but to perform. To flirt. To be seen. To tick the box. Because they already believe the lie that they're going to Hell anyway, so why try? The system is rigged. The path is narrow. The judges are unforgiving.

So, we sit there, week after week, carrying our own shame, pretending not to see the shame of others. We look holy, but we are hollow.

We were taught that the sanctuary was the house of the Lord. But I found no peace there. No love. No freedom. Just laws. Expectations. Gossip in the name of prayer. Judgement dressed in scripture.

It took years for me to realize the sanctuary I was looking for was not a building.

I Think God Is Gay

It was me.

It was always me.

The God I was told to find in a building was living quietly inside me. Waiting. Not to be worshipped through rules, but to be felt through love. Not to be reached through fear, but to be met in the stillness of knowing. The sanctuary is not stained glass and pulpits. The sanctuary is the place inside where you are honest with yourself. Where your wounds are safe. Where your questions are not sins, but songs. Where your truth is holy, even if it doesn't rhyme with the Bible verses, they used to silence you.

I carry my sanctuary with me now. And in that sanctuary, Angie dances freely in all her colour. Sam sings loudly, with liquor on his breath but freedom in his voice. Tholekile walks tall, her grandmother's

I Think God Is Gay

spirit beside her, powerful and wise. Melikhaya no longer hides, he speaks, he leads, he laughs without apology. They are not sinners. They are survivors. We are not the outcasts of the church. We are the church. And our sanctuary is finally sacred again.

I Think God Is Gay

A New Theology of Love

I believe God is Life. I believe Love is Life. I believe Life is Love.

These are not interchangeable words to me. They are sacred truths, stitched into the fabric of my skin, spoken by the breath I breathe, written into my tears, and held gently in every embrace I have ever given or received. These three, Life, Love, God, cannot exist without the other. You cannot touch one without feeling the vibration of all three.

For years, I tried to understand God through books, through sermons, through worn-out scriptures and old men's opinions. I sat on wooden pews and swallowed the fire of their words, trying not to choke. I listened to preachers tell me about a God that loves only some. I watched as they raised hands to the sky while casting stones

I Think God Is Gay

at the different, the broken, the queer. I watched as they turned children away from sanctuaries that should have saved them. I sat quietly when they condemned my kind. But my silence was never an agreement, it was survival.

Then, I left the church, not because I lost God, but because I was finally starting to feel Him.

I began to see Him in the most unexpected places. In the smile of a man with nothing left but hope. In the gentle hands of a lesbian couple caring for a dying parent. In the fire of a trans woman standing tall in a world that told her to shrink. In the soft apology of a mother who once couldn't understand her gay child but chose love over pride. And most of all, I began to feel Him inside myself, whispering truths that contradicted every sermon I'd ever heard:

I Think God Is Gay

"You are good. You are mine. You are not broken. You are not alone."

This is my theology: God is with us, in us, around us, regardless of what box the world wants to lock us in.

I have studied people. I have studied animals. I have studied trees, rivers, fire, and even silence. And I can tell you with no hesitation, God loves us all. He shows up in ways the Bible never documented, and church never taught.

I have seen sinners build homes for the homeless. I have watched addicts pull children from burning cars. I have seen sex workers pray for strangers and give their last coin to someone with less. I've watched men the church deemed "unclean" feed the starving with hands that never asked for praise.

I Think God Is Gay

This isn't the devil "rewarding bad behavior." This isn't God turning His back on the faithful. No, this is love, working in truth. This is God, not bound by the pages of an edited scripture but alive in the heartbeat of anyone who dares to care.

God is not a manipulator, rewarding the obedient and cursing the disobedient like a tyrant king. God is not sitting on a throne tallying your mistakes. He is not a jealous dictator demanding your worship or threatening your soul with eternal fire.

God is the quiet answer that comes before the prayer is even spoken.
God is the embrace you didn't ask for but desperately needed.
God is what you love so deeply it breaks you open and rebuilds you softer.

I Think God Is Gay

If your God only loves you because you fit a mould, then I ask you, do you love your God, or do you fear Him?

They told me my God couldn't exist. They told me the God I felt was a lie of my imagination. That I was making up something to feel better about being different, sinful, wrong.

But the God I feel speaks through my bones. The God I feel doesn't need a pulpit to be powerful.
The God I feel didn't write a book; He wrote me.

He wrote my laughter.
He wrote my silence.
He wrote my confusion, my desire, my heartbreak, and my healing.

When I look in the mirror, I no longer see someone unworthy of love, I see a chapter of God's own story.

I Think God Is Gay

That's why I can't stand silence anymore. That's why I had to write this book. Because I know there are others out there still trying to pray the gay away, still trying to fit into a church that never welcomed them, still trying to find God in places He has long since left. I am here to say: you are not the problem. Your love is not a mistake. You are not outside of God; you are *the very evidence of Him.*

There is no "wrong identity" in the kingdom of Love.

You cannot be too gay, too trans, too fluid, too unlabeled for the God I know. You cannot be too curious, too spiritual, too rebellious, or too tired. You cannot be too broken to be loved. The God I know doesn't ask for perfection. He doesn't ask for rules followed to the letter. He asks one thing: *do you love?*

I Think God Is Gay

That's the theology I live by now. That's the scripture I carry in my veins.

The old theologies were built to keep us out, built on fear, built on men's egos. But this new theology? This is built on love. It's built on the God who wept with the wounded, who dined with the hated, who forgave the worst and walked with the forgotten. The God who *became* the very thing people despised, human, and loved us anyway.

So no, I don't reject God.
I reject the boxes they tried to trap Him in.

I no longer need a church to validate my holiness.
I no longer need a priest to interpret my worth.
I no longer need a book to tell me what I already feel:

I am loved. I am divine. I am God's own creation.

I Think God Is Gay

And so are you.

Whoever you are, whatever they told you, however far you've wandered, however loud the voices of judgment, come home. Not to the building. Not to the preacher. Not to the dogma.

Come home to yourself.
Come home to the love you feel burning inside you.
That's God. That's your sanctuary. That's your truth.

A new theology of love begins here, right in your breath, in your heartbeat, in your story.

I Think God Is Gay

Finding My Tribe

We have one kind of Bible and hundreds of churches. One scripture, but countless interpretations. One God, but infinite human projections. And somehow, in all of that noise, confusion, shame, and rejection, I found a tribe. A people. A space where God wasn't feared or boxed in or weaponized. A space where I could just be.

Finding your tribe after exile is like finding air after drowning. And trust me, I was drowning for years. I had gone numb. I had stopped looking for God because I didn't think He wanted anything to do with someone like me. I had stopped trying to be holy because I was convinced, I was born already damned. But what no one tells you is that sometimes God stops showing up in churches so you can find Him in the people you choose to love.

I Think God Is Gay

My family is my church now. Not because we're bound by blood, but because we are bound by understanding. Acceptance. Truth. I chose them and they chose me, and isn't that what God is all about? Choosing each other even when we don't have to? I see God in them, in their patience, in the way they listen when I speak, in the way they hold space for my questions without panicking or preaching.

I see God in my best friend who lets me cry without trying to fix me. I see God in the young queer boy who told me that my words saved his life. I see God in the queer woman who still sings gospel in her car even after being excommunicated. I see God in every "I love you" that is said without hesitation or conditions. These people are not just my friends. They are not just allies. They are my sanctuary. My communion. My tribe.

I Think God Is Gay

Healing, I've learned, is not an event, it's a process. And sometimes it's an exorcism. Not of demons, but of shame. Of the voices that once said, "You are not worthy." Healing is the soft rebuke of the soul whispering back, "I am."

I won't lie to you and say it was easy. The church wounded me deeply. Not just with words, but with silence. With the way they looked away when I cried. With the way they made me sit in the back. With the sermons they preached *about me* but never *to me*. They buried me in doctrine and then blamed me for suffocating.

Some of us are still bleeding inside from churches that were supposed to be safe. I've spoken to people who tremble when they hear the word "pastor." Others who can't bring themselves to read the Bible without feeling shame crawl up their spine. And there are those who still pray in secret,

I Think God Is Gay

hoping God will answer without anyone else hearing.

We are the wounded ones. The ones carrying invisible scars from religious war zones. But here's the thing they didn't expect, wounded people still heal. Still sing. Still dance. Still build communities so full of love that heaven itself stands still to watch.

My tribe taught me that love isn't just the absence of hate, it's the active presence of care. It's the text message that says, "You were on my heart." It's the late-night drive to make sure you got home safe. It's the laughter over food. The prayer circle in the living room. The quiet hand on your back when words are too heavy. This is what church is supposed to be.

I've seen more holiness in queer support groups than in most mega churches. I've seen more miracles in therapy sessions than

I Think God Is Gay

in deliverance services. And I've seen God more clearly in the tears of my trans sister who just wants to be seen than I ever did in stained glass or pulpits.

You see, God was never confined to a religion. We did that. We put divinity in cages and called them doctrines. But the God I found after church… is wild. Free. Soft. Honest. And everywhere. Especially in the people who refuse to stop loving in a world determined to hate.

To those still looking for their tribe: don't give up. They are out there. People who will hold your truth and not flinch. People who will walk with you toward healing, even when the road is long. People who know that spirituality is not a building, it's a way of being. And if you haven't found them yet, start with this: be your own sanctuary. Speak to yourself kindly. Forgive yourself repeatedly. Love yourself fiercely. Because

I Think God Is Gay

every act of self-love is a prayer, and every prayer is a spark, and enough sparks make fire.

One day, someone will see that fire in you and say, "You too?" and you'll know, you've found home.

This is my gospel. My truth. My redemption. My sanctuary lives in people now. Not in marble floors or robes or incense. But in raw, flawed, extraordinary human beings who show up anyway. We may have been exiled from the buildings, but we found belongings in each other. And in that, I found God again, this time, for real.

I Think God Is Gay

The Day I Called God Queer (Gay)

I remember the day vividly. It wasn't marked by thunder or a burning bush. There was no choir of angels or a voice from the heavens. It was an ordinary day, the kind that slips by unnoticed. Yet, within its simplicity, I experienced a revelation that would forever change my understanding of the Divine.

I was sitting alone, reflecting on the tapestry of my life, the threads of joy, pain, rejection, and love. I thought about the countless times I had been told that who I am is incompatible with God. That my identity was a sin, an abomination, a deviation from the sacred. These words had been etched into my soul, leaving scars that no amount of prayer could heal. But on that day, as I sat in quiet contemplation, a thought emerged, gentle yet profound: *What if God is Gay?*

I Think God Is Gay

At first, the idea startled me. It felt blasphemous, heretical even. But as I allowed the thought to settle, it began to make sense. Not in the way that God has a sexual orientation, but in the essence of what "queer" represents, otherness, fluidity, the breaking of norms, the embrace of the marginalized. In that moment, I realized that the Divine has always been queer, gay, lesbian, or better yet, it has been the LQBTQI+ itself.

Throughout history, the Divine has defied human expectations. In many religious texts, God chooses the younger sibling over the elder, the barren woman to birth nations, the shepherd to lead a people. The Divine consistently aligns with the outsider, the unexpected, and the marginalized.

Consider the story of Jesus. Born to an unwed mother, in a stable, visited by shepherds and foreigners. He dined with

I Think God Is Gay

tax collectors, touched lepers, and spoke with women in public, actions that were radical and taboo in his cultural context. His life was a testament to queerness, not in sexuality, but in the radical embrace of the "other."

The word "Gay" has a complex history. Once wielded as a weapon to shame and ostracize, it has been reclaimed by many in the LGBTQ+ community as a badge of honor, a symbol of resilience and pride. To call God gay is to align the Divine with those who have been pushed to the margins, to affirm that the sacred is not confined to the halls of power but is present in the lives of those who live authentically, despite societal condemnation.

In my own journey, I have felt the Divine most profoundly in moments of vulnerability and authenticity. When I embraced my identity, when I loved

I Think God Is Gay

without fear, when I stood in solidarity with others who had been cast aside, I felt God's presence. Not the God of fire and brimstone, but the God of compassion, justice, and radical love.

This understanding of God as queer or lesbian, or the other has been a source of healing. It has allowed me to reconcile my faith with my identity, to see the sacred in my experiences, and to affirm that I am not an abomination, but a reflection of the Divine.

To see God as gay, bi, lesbian or queer is to challenge the traditional narratives that have been used to oppress and exclude. It is to recognize that the Divine is not bound by human constructs of gender, sexuality, or conformity. It is to affirm that all people, regardless of their identity, are made in the image of God.

I Think God Is Gay

This perspective invites us to create faith communities that are inclusive, affirming, and just. It calls us to dismantle systems of oppression and to build spaces where all can encounter the Divine without fear of rejection.

The day I thought God could be gay too was the day I found liberation. It was the day I saw the Divine not as a distant judge, but as an intimate presence that understands and embraces the fullness of who I am. It was the day I realized that my queerness is not a barrier to the sacred, but a pathway to deeper understanding.

In embracing the queerness of God, I have found a faith that is alive, dynamic, and transformative. A faith that speaks to the heart of who I am and invites me to live fully, love boldly, and walk in the truth of my identity. Many people have said those words as well, why not you?

I Think God Is Gay

Rewriting the Bible in My Skin

If it were up to me, I'd burn the Bible. Not out of hate, but out of heartbreak. I would tear the pages that told me I was an abomination. I would toss out the verses that were spat at me like bullets instead of being offered like bread. I would burn the Koran too, and every scripture used to cage the human soul in fear. But then again, I would be no better than the people who used those same books to burn me. To burn *us*.

So, I won't.

Not because I agree with them.

But because I know now that the power is not in the book, it's in the hands that hold it, in the mouths that preach it, and in the hearts that either weaponize or redeem it.

I will not rewrite the Bible on paper. I will rewrite it in my skin.

I Think God Is Gay

Every step I take will be a verse.
Every act of kindness will be a psalm.
Every breath I take while loving those they said were unworthy will be my scripture.

I will write the gospel of love on the way I hug.
I will preach the sermon of inclusion in how I listen.
I will carry grace in the way I speak to strangers.
When I walk into a room, no one will ask me how I do what I do.
They'll feel something.
They'll know, *there is God in me.*

Leviticus 18:22 "You shall not lie with a man as with a woman; it is an abomination."

The verse that's been sharpened like a dagger.

I Think God Is Gay

They quoted it to me at 14, when I couldn't explain why I didn't feel butterflies when my female friend smiled at me. They shouted it at me in youth services, with eyes that didn't see me, only the "sin" they assumed I carried. But none of them asked me what love felt like in my body. None of them saw the confusion, the pain, the nights I prayed to be different.

But let me ask: Was David an abomination when he said to Jonathan, *"Your love was more wonderful than that of women?"*
Was Ruth sinning when she told Naomi, *"Where you go, I go, and your people will be my people?"*
What if love, pure, soul-deep love, was never the sin?

What if the sin is in how we *use* scripture to kill what God is trying to heal?

I Think God Is Gay

So, I rewrote Leviticus. In my skin, it reads: "You shall not use love as a weapon. You shall not twist sacred affection into shame. You shall honour every heart that chooses love, even if it doesn't look like yours."

Genesis 19 – The Story of Sodom and Gomorrah

They said Sodom was destroyed because of homosexuality. They never told me it was about *inhospitality*. About rape, violence, and power. They forgot to mention that Lot offered his daughters to be gang-raped to protect strangers. They never preached that part.

They said God rained down fire for the gays. But when I read the text again, slowly, painfully, honestly, I saw something else. The people of Sodom were judged for cruelty, for their refusal to care for strangers, for their obsession with

I Think God Is Gay

domination and control. Not love. Not tenderness. Not queerness.

So, I rewrote Genesis 19 in the scars I carry from churches that locked their doors on me.

In my body, it reads:
"Woe to the city that rejects the broken. Woe to the holy who close their doors to the tired, the strange, the ones who walk alone. Sodom is not a place, it's a spirit. And that spirit lives not in queer bodies, but in the churches that forget to love."

Romans 1:26-27 "God gave them over to shameful lusts…"

They threw Paul's words at me like they were grenades, exploding any hope of being both holy and human. They said I exchanged natural relations for unnatural ones. But here's what they never taught: Paul was writing to a people surrounded by

I Think God Is Gay

idolatry, temple prostitution, and exploitative acts of dominance. It was about people using bodies as a means of power, not about people choosing to love.

No one ever asked Paul what he meant when he said, "*The greatest of these is love.*"

So, I rewrote Romans in the tenderness of my first kiss. It was slow, unsure, holy. There were no temples, no idols, no shame, just two trembling humans reaching for connection.

In my skin, it reads:
"God gives us over to shame only when we abandon love. But when we choose love, mutual, sacred, and consenting, God rejoices."

Deuteronomy 22:5 "A woman must not wear men's clothing, nor a man wear women's clothing…"

I Think God Is Gay

They laughed at the boy in heels. They whispered when the girl cut her hair short. They used this verse to build walls around gender like prisons. I wonder if they will ever build a prison for Gays only.

But I remember standing in front of the mirror, trying to understand my reflection. I didn't want to be male or female. I just wanted to be *me*. I remember a Sunday when I wore a shirt that made me feel seen. Someone said, "That's not appropriate for church." I smiled. But inside, I felt like God had dressed me Himself.

So, I rewrote Deuteronomy in the way I let my nephew wear nail polish for the first time, in the joy on his face when he saw he was still loved.

My version reads:
"Clothe yourself in what makes your soul

I Think God Is Gay

breathe. For God is not in fabric, but in freedom."

Corinthians 6:9 "Do not be deceived… neither the sexually immoral nor homosexuals… will inherit the kingdom of God."

They love this one. It's the final blow. The end of the debate. "See? Homosexuals don't get in. That's final." But I always asked, what is the *kingdom of God*? Is it heaven? Is it peace? Is it love? Jesus said, "The kingdom of God is within you." So maybe the ones who won't inherit it are not those who love differently, but those who choose *hate*.

Those who lie about God's heart.
Those who steal peace from queer children.
Those who refuse to sit beside someone who doesn't look or love like them.

I Think God Is Gay

So, I rewrote 1st Corinthians in the way I sit beside outcasts, hold space for the rejected, and refuse to hate myself anymore.

It reads:
"Do not be deceived: the kingdom belongs to those who love. Those who give, forgive, and embrace the least. The kingdom is within all, if we have the courage to claim it."

My Bible Has No Chapters, Only Moments
The Bible in my skin is written in memories. In the way my mother looked at me when I finally told her who or what I was, and she said, "You are my child. That's all that matters."

In the strangers who've wept on my shoulder because they thought they were going to Hell for being who they are. In the tears I've cried in silence, and the laughter that healed me afterward. In the quiet, still

I Think God Is Gay

voice that whispers when I am alone, "You are not a mistake."

That is my scripture.

So no, I won't burn the Bible. But I will *become* the Bible I wish existed.

The one that doesn't erase people. The one that doesn't condemn love. The one that knows God is not a punisher, but a presence. And when I die, I hope the story written in my life will be holy enough to save someone else from the fire. Not the one they preach about in Hell, but the one of shame, rejection, and silence.

I am rewriting the Bible in my skin. And I am finally free.

I Think God Is Gay

A Sin Is Not a Sin

They warned me not to say this.

They said I'd go to hell just for thinking it, let alone writing it down for the whole world to read. But how do you stay silent when your truth is burning through your ribs like fire? I'd rather risk your judgment than betray the clarity I've come to know. I'm not here to convince anyone. I'm simply here to tell the truth I found after the lies almost destroyed me.

I've come to this simple, soul-altering discovery: a sin is not a sin. At least not in the way they taught us. Not in the way we were made to fear ourselves into cages that smell like shame and obedience. You see, sin, real sin, is not about actions. It's about intention, harm, and disconnection. It's about the violence we do to each other's

I Think God Is Gay

humanity, not the choices we make to feel alive.

They told me being gay was a sin. They told me that loving someone the same gender as me was enough to erase me from heaven's book. But I've never felt more divine than when I loved someone in truth. When I held him and we cried together, healed together, built something sacred in secret, I swear, I felt God smiling. Not watching from above, but within. In us. Between us. Around us.

So, here I am saying it clearly, for those still trapped by fear and fire: being gay is not a sin.

Neither is dancing to music that makes your body feel like a cathedral. Neither is drinking wine on your balcony as you watch the sun rise and ask questions that no sermon has ever answered. Neither is

I Think God Is Gay

saying "no" to church because church has never said "yes" to you.

I used to be a male prostitute. That might shock you. It shocked me too, at first. But back then, it was one of the only ways I felt seen, touched, not just physically, but emotionally. I met women and men whose husbands treated them like prison guards. Women who just wanted to laugh, be heard, be desired. In those hotel rooms, I wasn't just a body. I was a mirror. I reflected their need for joy, for rebellion, for truth. That job taught me more about human nature than any Bible study ever did.

Was it right? Maybe not. Was it evil? Absolutely not.

Because that's what I've come to understand: wrong does not always mean wicked. And sin is not always what the church says it is. Sometimes, what they call

I Think God Is Gay

sin is really freedom in disguise, the kind of freedom that terrifies people who are addicted to control. Sometimes the only "sin" is daring to be fully, unapologetically yourself in a world that tells you to shrink or burn.

We have made sin into a political weapon, a religious leash, a tool to make others feel small. We've turned it into something that upholds power rather than protects people. But I've met so-called sinners who have given their last bread to the hungry, while saints pass by pretending not to see. I've seen drunkards who pray more honestly than sober pastors. I've seen love in places the Bible said was cursed.

And yes, I still believe in God. Deeply. But not the God of rules and rage. I believe in the God who created me with these desires, these questions, this fire in my chest. I

I Think God Is Gay

believe in the God who is love, and love cannot be sin.

Hurt? Yes. Abuse? Yes. Betrayal? Of course. To kill. Absolutely. Those are sins. Because they disconnect us from others and from ourselves. But to dance? To feel? To laugh too loud? To fall in love with the "wrong" person? To explore the deep wilderness of who you are?

Those are not sins.

They are part of the human experience, and the sooner we stop crucifying people for their humanity, the sooner we'll know what God's grace actually looks like. We're not sinners because we break rules. We become lost when we lose sight of love. Real love. Fierce, wild, untamed love that shows up when religion walks out the door.

So, no, I will not call myself a sinner for living my truth. I will not apologize for

I Think God Is Gay

choosing joy over tradition, authenticity over silence. If the road to hell is paved with people like me, lovers, dreamers, seekers, then I'm proud to walk it with them.

But I know better now.

We are not going to hell.

Hell is what we've been through. Hell is being told you're not good enough for God because of who you are. Hell is sitting in church pews while people talk about you like you're a disease. Hell is hiding your light because someone with a robe and microphone says you're too dirty to shine.

But my God, the God I know, the one who whispered to me in the library, in the arms of strangers, in the mirror after I cried myself to sleep, that God is not sending anyone like me to hell.

That God is burning inside me, helping me unlearn every lie that chained me to fear.

I Think God Is Gay

So, no. A sin is not a sin.

A sin is forgetting who you are. A sin is treating someone as less than a human. A sin is hiding your soul so the crowd won't boo. A sin is teaching others to hate in the name of love.

If you've ever been called a sinner, read this and breathe again.

You are not broken. You are not damned. You are not unworthy of love, light, or God.

You are human and holy, exactly as you are.

I Think God Is Gay

Who Cares About Afterlife?

I mean who, really? Who cares about the afterlife? the unknown.

No one's ever been there. No one has come back with proof, and yet, somehow, the fear of what lies beyond this life has become more powerful than the life we're living right now. Yes, it's natural to wonder. Curiosity isn't a sin. But why should we live in fear, shrinking ourselves and following rigid rules, because of something we don't know and cannot control?

We are all going to die one day. That should not terrify us, it should awaken us. It should teach us to live, fully and unapologetically, while we still can. To laugh loud, to dance wild, to love without permission. This life is not a waiting room. It is the moment. And we're wasting it chasing tickets to a heaven no one can confirm.

I Think God Is Gay

Instead of fearing the next life, why don't we fix this one?

Let us come together, really come together, and end the cycles of tears, suffering, poverty, corruption, and hate. Let's stop using religion to divide and start using love to unite. Let's rebuild humanity, promote compassion, and look at each other not as sinners or saints, but simply as people. If we truly believe that no one is greater than the other in the eyes of God, then let us live like we believe it. Let us see one another the same way, with equal worth, equal grace, equal need for healing.

This nation, this world, it could be something beautiful. But we're distracted. We're obsessed with the unknown and paralyzed by fear. We're trapped in a world of "what ifs" and "am I good enough?" while life passes us by. On this earth, people are working themselves to death for a

I Think God Is Gay

chance at heaven. People who are blessed simply by being alive are weighed down by fear of what comes after.

Christians fight each other over the "right way" to reach God. And here I am, simply voicing what my soul has discovered. Please, my brothers and sisters, calm your hearts. Breathe. God did not create us just to throw us into the hands of devils. We are here now. This is our time, our one, fragile, beautiful chance. Let us not waste it worrying about death when we haven't even learned how to live.

And yet… the world is crumbling.

Men are becoming monsters. Our nation is decaying from the inside. Our education system is collapsing. Our youth are obsessed with image, luxury, and popularity, chasing illusions while wisdom fades into dust. Our government is a

I Think God Is Gay

sanctuary for criminals. Our churches are built on hypocrisy and, at worst, abuse. And in the middle of all this, people are still obsessing over the afterlife.

What the actual hell is going on?

We don't care which political party rules; we just want leaders, real ones. We don't care about celebrities, we want helpers, healers, people who care whether the hungry eat and the lost are found. We're not begging for a seat in a church; we're begging for assurance that God still hears us.

But who am I to say this?

I'm just a gay, bi, homosexual guy trying to stay alive in a dark, unforgiving land.

Once, a man looked me in the eye and said my voice would never matter in this world. He told me my soul was headed straight for hell.

I Think God Is Gay

He was a church leader. A man who had never seen heaven or hell but somehow spoke with authority about who deserves glory and who deserves fire. His words didn't come from God; they came from fear and ignorance dressed in sacred robes.

It happened on a Sunday. We were invited to speak, to share what God had done for us. The testimonies flowed like poetry. A man confessed he'd been a terrible husband, but that God had redeemed him. A woman stood trembling, admitting to a life of sleeping with married men, but hopeful that grace would reach her too. Some were clapped for. Others weren't.

And then it was my turn.

My knees shook. My heartbeat echoed in my ears. I could barely hold the microphone. I took a deep breath and began:

I Think God Is Gay

"My name is Sipho Ellen Tshaka. I'm from Bizana in the Eastern Cape. I don't know if I belong here. But I came because I heard what God has done in your lives. And I want to say… God has blessed me too. I may not live like most of you. I may not believe like most of you. But I know God's love. I live it. I feel it. And yes, I'm gay. And I know God loves me, too."

Silence. Like fog settling over the congregation. Whispering. Fidgeting. Eyes avoiding mine.

I had said too much. And many weren't ready.

The service continued. No one responded to my words. No one clapped. And when it ended, I was asked to stay behind.

The pastor looked me in the eye, surrounded by his elders, and said:

I Think God Is Gay

"My son, your voice will never matter in this world. And you are going straight to hell if you do not change. You offend God by being gay and still dare enter His service."

I stood frozen, my heart pounding, my body on the verge of collapse.

If it had been God saying that to me, maybe I could have accepted it. But it wasn't. It was just a man. A man like me, flawed, flesh and blood, broken. A man who had never seen the afterlife but spoke of it like he owned it. Like he had the power to condemn souls.

Still, it didn't shake my truth.

I am a gay man who knows the love of God. And because of that, I no longer fear the afterlife. Because I live with love now. I walk in truth now. That's all I need.

But it's not easy.

I Think God Is Gay

Most people don't want to hear this truth. Most people would rather I disappear than accept that God might love me just as I am.

I Think God Is Gay

If God Is Love, Then God Is...

There was a time when I sat in churches with clenched fists and a trembling heart, afraid to breathe too loudly in case the holy silence broke and exposed me. I feared being found out, not for something I did, but for something I was. For something I *am*. I walked into sanctuaries searching for peace, only to find war declared on my very existence. I listened to sermons that spoke of hell more than they spoke of healing. I watched pastors pound pulpits and call it passion, even when it was poison. I saw love weaponized, and God held hostage behind tradition and fear. This book was born from that place, from exile, from confusion, and from the long, slow crawl toward wholeness.

I wrote this because I needed to. Because if I didn't, I feared the silence would finish what the shame started. This book is my

I Think God Is Gay

altar, my scream, my healing. It's my prayer for every person who was ever made to feel unworthy in the name of religion. It's for the child who looked in the mirror and whispered, *God, if I am wrong, why did You make me this way?* It's for the adults still carrying the weight of that question in their chest like a ticking bomb. I wrote this to say: you are not alone. You are not broken. And you are not an abomination. You are beloved, and your existence is not a mistake, it's a message.

For years, I begged God to make me different. I prayed the gay away. I fasted, cried, confessed, and punished myself with holy discipline, hoping to become palatable to a divine being I thought demanded perfection. But no matter how hard I tried, God wouldn't disappear from the parts of me they told me were damned. That's when I started to realize that maybe God was

I Think God Is Gay

never the problem, maybe it was the image of God that was flawed. Maybe the real sin wasn't in who I loved, or how I dressed, or what I felt. Maybe the real sin was in creating a theology that makes people choose between their truth and their belonging.

I've watched people, beautiful, kind, queer, broken, gay, bi, lesbian, healed, searching, walk away from faith because they were never given the space to meet a God big enough to hold all of them. And the truth is, many of them didn't walk away from God, they walked away from the version of God that was weaponized against them. They left the doors of buildings that claimed to represent love but taught them to hate themselves. And so, they began the sacred journey of unlearning. Of reclaiming. Of remembering who they were before the

I Think God Is Gay

world told them who they had to be to earn love.

Through all this, I began to understand something I was never told in church: that God is not outside of me, judging my footsteps from a distance. God is within me. God is in my breath, in my resilience, in my survival. God is in my laughter, my softness, my silence, my rage. God is in the gay child finding their voice, in the trans parent tucking their kid in at night, in the gay teenager writing poetry under the covers. God is in the broken, the healing, the curious, the strange, the outcast. God is not limited by the labels we use to exclude each other. God is love. And if that's true, then anything outside of love cannot be God.

I know what it means to be exiled from a place you once called holy. I know what it feels like to sit in a church chairs surrounded by people and still feel

I Think God Is Gay

completely alone. I know the ache of wanting to belong and the shame of believing you never truly will. I know what it's like to dress differently, speak softly, avoid eye contact, just to avoid suspicion. But I also know the power of choosing your truth. I know the holiness of walking out of places that shrink you and into spaces where your soul can breathe. I know the divine in chosen families, in late-night conversations, in holding hands with someone who sees you. I know now that I carry God within me, and I no longer need permission to be sacred.

This book is a mirror. For you, the reader, I hope it reflects something you've always felt but couldn't say out loud. I hope it disrupts the narratives that kept you in hiding. I hope it awakens something ancient and unbreakable in your bones. I want you to know that your pain is valid, your story

I Think God Is Gay

is powerful, and your existence is necessary. I hope this book offers you a new theology, a theology of love that doesn't ask you to choose between God and your truth. One that doesn't silence your identity or make you apologize for being real. One that whispers to you, even in your darkest hours: *You are enough. You've always been enough. You were made in the image of Love Itself.*

So, if God is love, then God is the embrace after the confession. God is the quiet strength it takes to come out, to come home to yourself. God is the courage to question. God is the patient in healing. God is the voice that says, "I still choose you," when the world turns away. God is not a threat. God is not a weapon. God is not the shame you were taught to carry like a cross. God is present. God is warmth. God is truth. God

I Think God Is Gay

is the fire in your belly and the peace in your chest.

I'll leave you with this: Do not be afraid to love yourself deeply. Do not be afraid to question, to wrestle, to rebuild. Do not be afraid to walk away from what hurts you, even if it wears a holy name. The road to spiritual freedom is not paved with guilt, it is made of grace, tears, laughter, and radical self-acceptance. And you will walk that road in your own time, at your own pace. Just don't forget: you're not walking it alone.

If God is love, then God is you. God is me. God is every misfit, every queer soul, every hurting heart that has ever longed to be seen. If God is love, then God is not far off or far away. God is here. Now. In the mess, in the questions, in the healing. And if God is love, *really* love, then God has never once left you. Not even for a second.

www.ingramcontent.com/pod-product-compliance
Lightning Source LLC
Chambersburg PA
CBHW032047040426
42449CB00007B/1016